# Are You My Cat?

by Marybeth Mataya
Illustrated by Matthew Williams

Content Consultant:
Gerald Brecke
Doctor of Veterinary Medicine

magic wagon

Are You My Pet?

# visit us at www.abdopublishing.com

Published by Magic Wagon, a division of the ABDO Publishing Group, 8000 West 78th Street, Edina, Minnesota 55439. Copyright © 2009 by Abdo Consulting Group, Inc. International copyrights reserved in all countries. All rights reserved. No part of this book may be reproduced in any form without written permission from the publisher.

Looking Glass Library™ is a trademark and logo of Magic Wagon.

Printed in the United States.

Text by Marybeth Mataya
Illustrations by Matthew Williams
Edited by Jill Sherman
Interior layout and design by Emily Love
Cover design by Emily Love

**Library of Congress Cataloging-in-Publication Data**
Mataya, Marybeth.
 Are you my cat? / by Marybeth Mataya ; illustrated by Matthew Williams ; content consultant, Gerald Brecke.
    p. cm. — (Are you my pet?)
Includes index.
ISBN 978-1-60270-242-4
1.  Cats—Juvenile literature.  I. Williams, Matthew, 1971- ill. II. Title.
SF445.7.M26 2009
636.8—dc22
                            2008003639

*Note to Parents/Guardians:*
*This book can help you teach your child how to be a kind, responsible cat owner. Even so, a child will not be able to handle all the responsibilities of having a pet, so we are glad that you will oversee the responsibility. Adults, with the exception of pregnant women, should clean the litter. Also, neutering or spaying your cat is a key step in helping reduce pet overpopulation and the number of homeless and abused pets.*

# Table of Contents

## Is a Cat the Right Pet for Me?

Do you like to cuddle? Do you like soft fur? Then a cat may be the right pet for you!

Cats are very loving animals. They also need a lot of love and care.

Before you bring a cat home, have everyone in your family spend time with the cat. Many people are allergic to cats. They get rashes, watery eyes, and stuffy noses. You do not want to find out that you are allergic to cats after you have one!

**Pet Fact:**

*Just like you, cats need checkups. After you get your cat, bring it to a veterinarian.*

## *How Old Should My Cat Be?*

Kittens are young cats. They are cute and playful. But kittens are usually more work than a cat. Kittens need to be fed often. They need to be trained. And they need to be watched all the time.

8

**Pet Fact:**

*Animal shelters take care of animals without homes. They have many kittens and cats that need to find loving homes.*

9

## What Kind of Cat Would Be Best?

Cats come in many kinds, or breeds. Most pet cats are a mix of different breeds. Some cats have long hair. Some cats have short hair. Cats with long hair need a lot of brushing. They also shed.

Each cat has its own personality. Before you choose a cat, watch how it acts. Does it meow at you? Does it like to play? Gently hold the cat. If it hisses or scratches, it is not the right cat for you. It may be the right cat for someone else.

**Pet Fact:**
*Some cat breeds have fun names, such as Ragdoll or Australian Mist.*

## What Does My Cat Need?

Every cat needs a scratching post, a soft bed, a food bowl, and a water bowl. Cats need clean water every day. A cat also needs a litter box. This is the box the cat will use as its bathroom.

Cats love to play. You can buy your cat safe toys to play with. Ask your veterinarian for a list of good toys. You will also need a cat carrier for visits to the veterinarian.

**Pet Fact:**
*String and ribbon are not safe toys. Cats can swallow them and get sick.*

15

# What Should I Feed My Cat?

You should feed your cat good cat food. If you do not, your cat could become sick. A veterinarian can help you choose the food. Feed your cat a little twice each day. A kitten needs to eat more often.

Do not feed your cat scraps from your plate. The salt and fat in table scraps can make your cat sick. Keep your cat away from bones, chocolate, garlic, salt, onions, coffee, raisins, and grapes. Even milk can give your cat an upset stomach. But, you can give your pet a cat treat once in a while.

**Pet Fact:**
*Make sure your cat's food dish is not near its litter box. Otherwise, your cat may not use one of them.*

## How Do I Get to Know My Cat?

When your cat meets you, let it smell your hand. Spend time talking to your cat, and pet it gently.

Some people think cats do not need company. They do! Cats get lonesome when they are left alone all day. They get cranky and act badly to show you they are mad.

**Pet Fact:**
*Purring means your cat is happy. A happy cat may also rub against you or gently push its paws against you.*

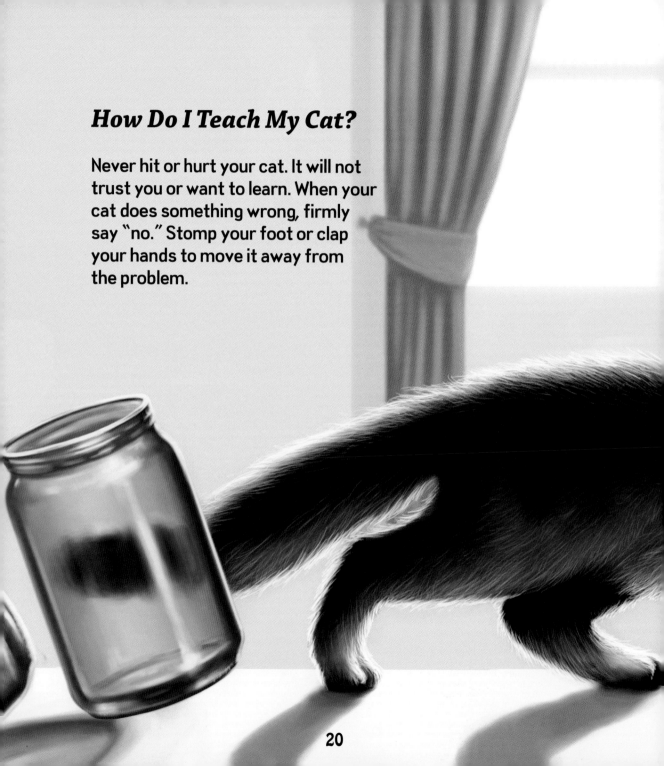

## How Do I Teach My Cat?

Never hit or hurt your cat. It will not trust you or want to learn. When your cat does something wrong, firmly say "no." Stomp your foot or clap your hands to move it away from the problem.

Reward your cat when it does something good. Say "good kitty" with a happy voice. Give it hugs and cat treats. Always hold your cat with one arm under its rear and one under its front paws. Never pick it up by the scruff of its neck.

**Pet Fact:**

*If your cat's ears and tail are up, it is paying attention.*

# How Do I Keep My Cat Clean?

Cats like to be clean. To stay clean, cats lick themselves. This is called grooming.

Your cat still needs to be brushed. The poop in the litter box also needs to be scooped out once a day. The box needs to be emptied and cleaned once a week. A cat will not use a dirty litter box. You can help an adult with these chores, but you should wear cleaning gloves.

### Pet Fact:

*Used kitty litter has a lot of germs. Do not flush it down the toilet. It could carry germs into rivers and harm wildlife.*

# How Do I Keep My Cat Safe?

Keep your cat indoors! This keeps your cat safe from cars, fleas, ticks, and many illnesses.

Put a collar with a tag on your cat in case it slips through the door. The tag should have your cat's name and your name, address, and phone number.

Watch what your cat eats. Ask an adult to put away cleaning bottles and move houseplants. If your cat looks sick, visit the veterinarian.

### Pet Fact:

*Bring your cat to the veterinarian for a checkup each year. If your trained cat pees or poops someplace strange, it may be telling you that it is sick.*

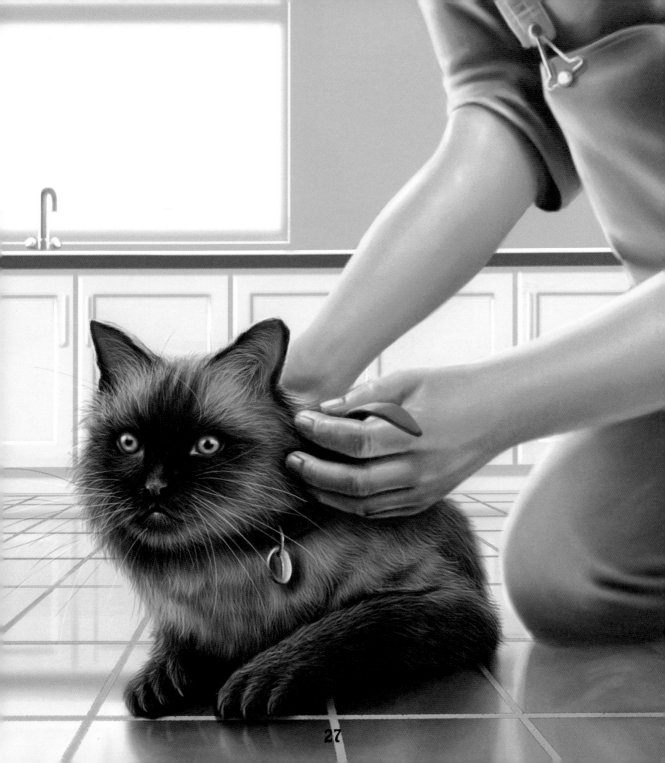

## How Do I Stay Safe?

Pay attention to your cat and its moods. If its ears and tail are back or twitching or if the cat is hissing, back away.

If your cat runs from you, do not chase or grab it. Sit and wait until your cat comes to you. And most importantly, enjoy this wonderful new friend!

**Pet Fact:**
*Cats often live between 14 and 20 years.*

## Words to Know

*allergic*—to have a bad reaction from being around something.

*animal shelter*—a safe place for homeless animals.

*breed*—a specific kind of animal within a species.

*groom*—to clean oneself to stay healthy.

*litter box*—the place where a cat goes to the bathroom.

*rash*—a red area on a person's skin due to allergy or illness.

*shed*—to lose extra hair.

*train*—to teach an animal rules or tricks.

*veterinarian*—an animal doctor.

## Further Reading

Dennis-Bryan, Kim. *Kitten Care: How to Look After Your Pet*. New York: DK
    Publishing, 2004.
Evans, Mark. *Kitten: ASPCA Pet Care Guide*. New York: DK Children, 2001.
Hanson, Anders. *Cuddly Cats*. Perfect Pets series. Edina, MN: ABDO
    Publishing, 2007.
Wilkins, Kelli A. *Cats: Animal Planet Pet Care Library*. Neptune City, NJ: TFH
    Publications, 2007.

## On the Web

To learn more about cats, visit ABDO Publishing Company on the World Wide
Web at **www.abdopublishing.com**. Web sites about cats are featured on our
Book Links page. These links are routinely monitored and updated to provide
the most current information available.

# Index